JOELITO'S BIG DECISION

LA GRAN DECISIÓN DE JOELITO

PRAISE FOR *JOELITO'S BIG DECISION/LA GRAN DECISIÓN DE JOELITO*

Joelito is a **CALIFORNIA READS** 2016-2017 RECOMMENDED BOOK

"We are happy to promote and distribute *Joelito's Big Decision*—a wonderful new picture book for children on the rights of workers. Thank you Ann Berlak for writing such a needed book." **Teaching For Change**

"An important story that introduces a current event... Recommended for libraries looking to expand social justice and bilingual collections." **Selenia Paz, Helen Hall Library, League City, TX School Library Journal**

"My current favorite book about activism is *Joelito's Big Decision*....a story that is both explicitly about a particular action, but also about fairness, and a child's choices." **Innosanto Nagara, author/illustrator of *A is for Activist*.**

"A children's book was written about the #FightFor15. It's one of the best things we've seen. Check it out and support the author." **Fight for $15 NY**

"This is a terrific read for kids, one that will teach them about fairness and responsibility in this era of growing inequality and injustice. I recommend it highly." **Sonia Nieto, Professor Emerita, School of Education, UMass Amherst**

"This is a wonderful book taking on a timely topic... Great story, beautifully told, terrific illustrations, and bilingual... wonderful!" **Reach and Teach**

"This book will open important conversations about the role of workers in the food systems and communities in which we live." **Diana Cohn, author, *Si Se Puede***

"While world attention is focused on labor's monumental "Fight for 15" struggle, Joelito's Big Decision/ La Gran Decisión de Joelito couldn't have been published at a better time... Kudos to all involved in this gigantically important little book." **De Colores: The Raza Experience in Books for Children**

JOELITO'S BIG DECISION
LA GRAN DECISIÓN DE JOELITO

Written by Ann Berlak

Illustrations by Daniel Camacho

Translation by José Antonio Galloso

Published by Hard Ball Press.
Information available at: www.hardballpress.com
ISBN:978-0-9862400-9-6
Story by Ann Berlak
Illustrations by Daniel Camacho
Translation José Antonio Galloso
Cover design by Innosanto Nagara
Editing services by Maria Reyes
Book design by D. Bass.

Library of congress Cataloging-in-publication data
1. Family life – fiction. 2. Immigrant life – fiction. 3. Fast food workers – fiction. 4. Social justice. 5. Hispanic-Americans.

Dedication

This book is lovingly dedicated to the families of workers who toil in restaurants, chain stores, car washes, and other industries that fail to pay a living wage.

Este libro está dedicado con amor a las familias de los trabajadores que, en restaurantes, cadenas de almacenes, lavado de autos, y otras industrias, no reciben un salario digno.

Joelito awakened to the smell of chorizo frying. After a dreamy minute he realized it was Friday, his favorite day. He loved Fridays because Mama and Papa took him and his sister Alma to MacMann's for burgers every Friday, rain or shine.

From his window he could see the twelve-foot high plastic head of Smiling Sam MacMann across the street. On their car trip to Los Angeles they'd counted fifteen Smiling Sams. He supposed there were thousands of MacMann's across the planet.

El olor del chorizo en la sartén despertó a Joelito. Estaba aún entre el sueño y la realidad cuando cayó en la cuenta de que era su día favorito. Le encantaban los viernes porque mamá y papá lo llevaban con su hermana Alma a comer hamburguesas en el restaurante MacMann's.

Joelito miró a través de la ventana que la enorme cabeza de plástico del Sonriente Sam MacMann lo miraba desde la ascera de enfrente. Una vez había ido en auto a Los Ángeles y en el camino había contado quince Sam Sonrientes, todos iguales, de doce pies de alto, y hechos de plástico. Cerró los ojos y se imaginó que había miles de MacManns en todo el planeta.

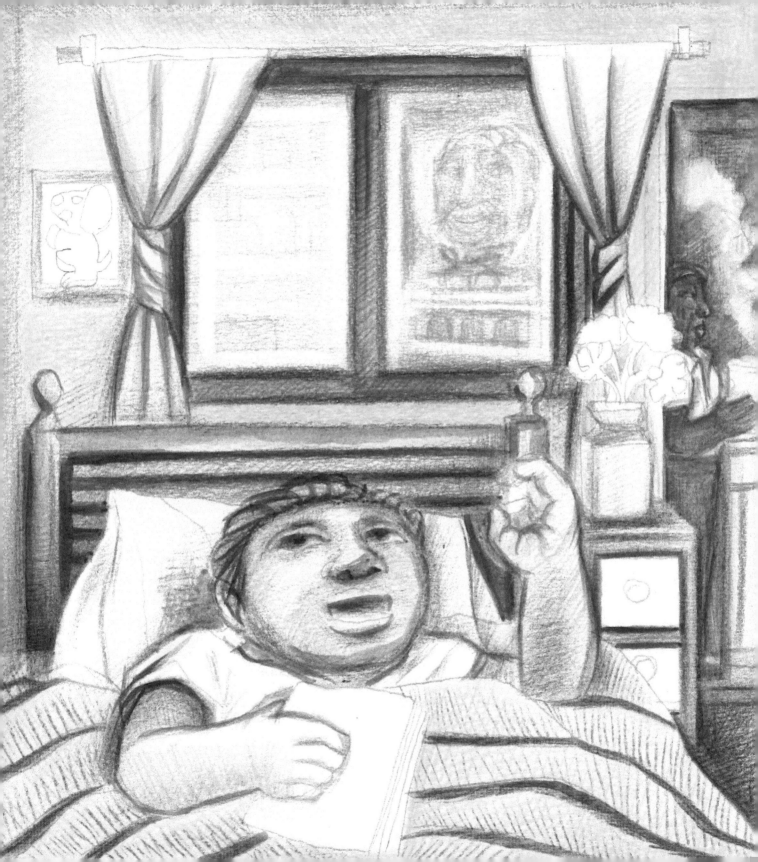

At three o'clock Joelito and his best friend Brandon waited outside the third grade classroom for their younger sisters. Alma came out with Brandon's sister Kayla, who was crying.

"Brandon, someone stole your sister's backpack!" said Alma. "We looked everywhere!"

"I loved that backpack," Kayla said. "It was practically new."

"Don't worry, Kayla," Joelito said. "There are others just like it at the store."

"Joelito Sanchez, you don't understand anything!" Kayla replied. "I won't be getting another one for a very long time!"

A las tres de la tarde, Joelito y Brandon, su mejor amigo, esperaban a sus hermanitas afuera del salón de tercer grado. Alma y Kayla salieron juntas. Kayla estaba llorando.

–¡Brandon! –dijo Alma–, alguien se robó la mochila de tu hermana. ¡La buscamos por todos lados y no la encontramos!

–Yo adoraba esa mochila –dijo Kayla–, era prácticamente nueva.

–No te preocupes, Kayla –dijo Joelito–, hay otras iguales en la tienda.

–Joelito Sánchez, no entiendes nada –respondió Kayla–. No volveré a tener otra en mucho tiempo.

The four walked home through a misty rain. When Joelito and Alma reached their building, they said good-bye to their friends and walked upstairs to their apartment.

Joelito was still thinking about Kayla's backpack. Once he'd left his backpack on the bus and Papa took him to buy another one the next day.

At six o'clock Joelito and Alma heard their parents coming home. "Ready to go?" Papa asked.

"Ready for my burger!" said Joelito.

Los cuatro amigos caminaron de regreso a casa bajo una delicada llovizna. Al llegar a la puerta de su edificio, Joelito y Alma se despidieron de sus amigos y subieron al departamento donde vivían.

Joelito se había quedado pensando en la mochila de Kayla. Una vez, él había olvidado su mochila en el autobús y su papá lo llevó al día siguiente a comprar una nueva.

A las seis de la tarde, como todos los viernes, Alma escuchó a sus papás entrar al departamento.

–¿Ya están listos para salir? –preguntó el papá desde la sala.

–¡Listo! –dijo Joelito.

As they stepped outside, Papa pointed across the street. "Something's happening at MacMann's. Let's check it out."

Joelito had never seen MacMann's parking lot so crowded. There were people of all ages and colors. They smiled at each other as if they all were friends. Many carried cardboard signs. Some signs said LOW PAY IS NOT OK, SI SE PUEDE or STRIKE FOR 15.

From the rooftop Smiling Sam gazed down upon the scene.

–¡Algo está pasando en MacMann's! –dijo el papá al salir del edificio–. ¡Vamos a ver!

Al otro lado de la calle, el estacionamiento de MacMann's estaba lleno de gente. Joelito nunca había visto algo así, tantas personas reunidas, de todos los colores y de todas las edades. Le llamó la atención ver cómo se trataban entre ellos, con mucha amabilidad, con sonrisas en las caras. Muchos cargaban pancartas. Algunas decían: ¡LOS SUELDOS BAJOS NO ESTÁN BIEN!, ¡Sí SE PUEDE!, ¡HUELGA POR LOS 15!:

Más arriba, de plástico, de tres metros y medio de alto, el Sonriente Sam MacMann contemplaba la escena.

Joelito and Alma peeked through the crowd at the restaurant door. They could see that MacMann's was packed inside, but no one was standing in line or eating at tables.

They heard mama calling, "Joelito and Alma Sanchez! Come here!" but they kept moving towards the restaurant door until Mama called again. Then they turned around.

At that moment Joelito saw Brandon, Kayla and their parents, Mr. and Mrs. Thomas standing together and holding signs.

Abriéndose paso entre la gente, Joelito y Alma llegaron a la puerta del restaurante. Estaba lleno de gente, pero no había nadie haciendo fila ni comiendo en las mesas.

–¡Joelito! ¡Alma! –escucharon ambos la voz de su madre pero la curiosidad pudo más que la obediencia y siguieron avanzando.

–¡Joelito y Alma Sánchez! ¡Vengan aquí! –gritó la mamá con tal firmeza que los chicos supieron que había que regresar.

En ese momento Joelito vio a Brandon, Kayla y los señores Thomas, sus padres. Cada uno sostenía una pancarta.

Mr. and Mrs. Thomas cooked burgers at MacMann's. They had worked at a factory until the factory closed down. Then the family moved from their house with a backyard into a one-bedroom apartment, and they had to give their dog, Cookie, away. Brandon still talked about how much he loved Cookie.

Los padres de Kayla y Brandon se encargaban de cocinar las hamburguesas de MacMann's. Antes habían trabajado en una fábrica hasta que ésta cerró. Entonces la familia tuvo que mudarse a un departamento de una sola recámara, y tuvieron que regalar a su perrito Cookie. Brandon todavía habla de cuánto quería a Cookie.

"What's going on?" asked Joelito.

Mrs. Thomas said, "We're picketing to let people know MacMann's doesn't pay us enough to support our families. We want fifteen dollars an hour, though even that's not enough. We should earn enough so we can pay our bills *and* go on a family vacation."

Joelito thought about Kayla's missing back-pack. No wonder she'd been so upset. He guessed Brandon's parents never came to soccer games because they had to work Saturdays at MacMann's.

–¿Qué está pasando? –quiso saber Joelito.

–Qué bueno que lo preguntas, Joelito –respondió la señora Thomas–. Hemos organizado esta protesta para que la gente sepa que MacMann's no les paga a sus trabajadores un sueldo justo. Lo que pagan en MacMann's no nos alcanza siquiera para mantener a nuestras familias. Queremos que nos paguen quince dólares la hora aunque ni siquiera eso es suficiente. Todo trabajador debería ganar lo suficiente como para poder pagar sus cuentas y tener unas vacaciones de vez en cuando.

Joelito pensó en Kayla. Finalmente pudo entender por qué ella estaba tan triste y preocupada con la pérdida de su mochila. Pensó que lo más probable era que los padres de Brandon y Kayla nunca podían ir a los partidos de fútbol porque tenían que trabajar los sábados en MacMann's.

"Why doesn't Akila just pay the workers more?" Alma asked. Akila, who used to babysit for them, was a manager at MacMann's.

Mr. Thomas answered, "Akila doesn't decide how much to pay the workers. When someone buys a MacMann's burger anywhere on earth, a lot of that money goes into Mr. MacMann's bank account. He decides how much of that money to pay the workers and the managers and how much to keep for himself."

–¿Por qué Akila no decide subirle el sueldo a los trabajadores? –Preguntó Alma–. Yo sé que ella lo haría.

Akila, que antes era la niñera que los cuidaba, ahora era la gerente de MacMann's.

–Es que Akila no decide cuánto se le paga a los trabajadores –respondió el señor Thomas.

–Cada vez que alguien compra una hamburguesa en cualquier MacMann's del mundo, mucho dinero llega a la cuenta bancaria del señor MacMann. Él decide cuánto de ese dinero se usa para pagar a los trabajadores y a los gerentes, y con cuánto se va a quedar él.

A small crowd had gathered around them listening. Mr. Thomas continued, "It's a math problem, brother. One year Sam MacMann was paid nine million dollars. I'd have to work *five hundred years* to earn as much as Sam earns in one year. Mr. MacMann's bank account is bursting, and we can't pay the rent. He has way more money than he needs because he pays the workers so little."

La gente, interesada en lo que el señor Thomas decía, se empezó a agrupar alrededor de ellos:

–Es un problema de matemáticas, compañeros –continuó el señor Thomas–. Un año, Sam MacMann recibió nueve millones de dólares. Tendría que trabajar quinientos años para ganar lo que Sam gana en un año. La cuenta bancaria del señor MacMann está repleta y nosotros ni siquiera podemos pagar la renta. Tiene mucho más dinero de lo que necesita porque paga muy poco a sus empleados.

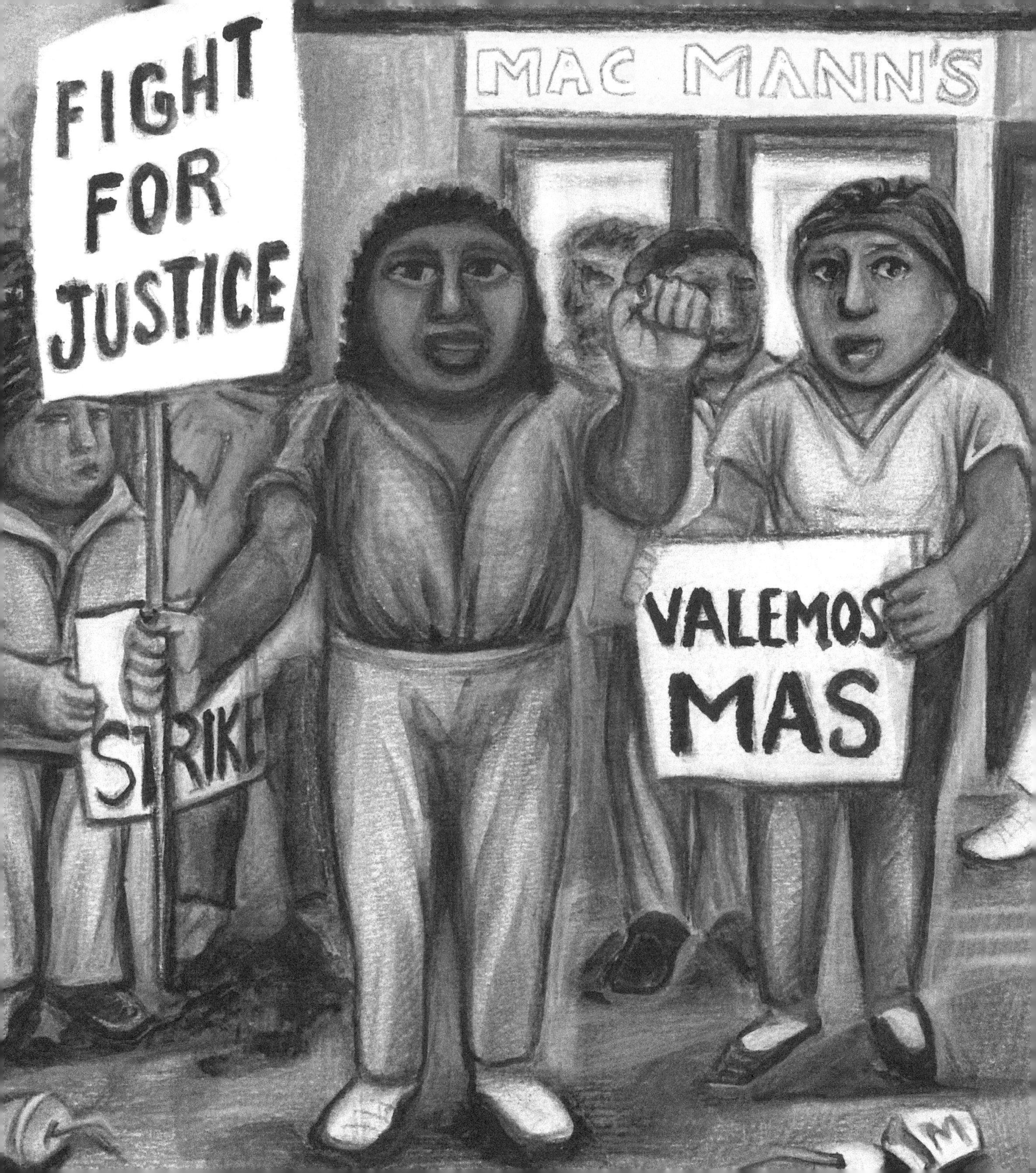
FIGHT FOR JUSTICE
MAC MANN'S
VALEMOS MAS
STRIKE
M

A TV reporter held a microphone in front of Mr. Thomas and asked, "Won't MacMann's have to charge more for hamburgers if they pay the workers more?" His answer would be on TV tonight.

"Sam MacMann has a billion dollars in the bank," Mr. Thomas said. "He could easily pay workers more without raising prices."

Joelito's stomach growled. He glanced back at MacMann's, where the burgers were frying on a grill. They smelled *so* good.

Un reportero de televisión levantó un micrófono frente al señor Thomas y preguntó:

–Esto es para el noticiero de esta noche. Díganos, señor, ¿para que MacMann's pueda pagar los quince dólares que ustedes piden, tendrá que subirle el precio a las hamburguesas?

–Sam MacMann tiene un billón de dólares en el banco –respondió el señor Thomas–, si tuviera la voluntad de hacerlo, nos podría subir el sueldo mañana sin tener que cobrar un centavo más por hamburguesa.

De pronto, el estómago de Joelito gruño. Miró hacia el interior del restaurante, donde cocinaban las hamburguesas sobre la parrilla. Olían bien ricas.

"Joelito," Mama said. "If we ate at MacMann's tonight, your abuelos would turn over in their graves. When your uncles and I were young, we worked from dawn to dusk picking grapes in the sizzling sun. Pesticides. No bathrooms in the fields. Picking grapes hardly paid enough to feed us! We were always hungry. Demonstrating to be treated more fairly saved your abuelos' lives."

–Joelito –le dijo su mamá–, si esta noche comiéramos hamburguesas en MacMann's tus abuelos se retorcerían en sus tumbas. Ellos trabajaron muy duro en los campos de uvas y en condiciones terribles, sin baños, expuestos a los pesticidas venenosos que rociaban sobre los viñedos. Tus abuelos recogían uvas de sol a sol con la intención de darnos una vida mejor a tus tíos y a mí; pero ese trabajo, a pesar de lo duro que era, no les pagaba lo suficiente para siquiera alimentarnos bien y siempre estábamos con hambre. Las protestas a favor de un trato más justo para los trabajadores del campo les salvó la vida a tus abuelos.

"OK," said Joelito, "Let's go to Powerburger's instead."

"Can't eat there either," said Mr. Thomas. "The workers at Powerburger's are demonstrating, too. Low paid workers are demonstrating all over the world today."

"Where *can* we eat?" asked Alma.

A short, grandmotherly woman said, "Try Cocina Las Ollitas on 18th, they have great food and the workers get paid fairly. There's no Mr. MacMann getting richer every time someone buys a burger."

"Sounds good to me," Mama said.

–Estoy de acuerdo –dijo Joelito–. Mejor vamos a Powerburger.

–Lo siento Joelito, pero no van a poder ir ahí tampoco –dijo el señor Thomas–. Los trabajadores de Powerburger también están protestando. Hoy es un día de protesta para los trabajadores mal pagados del mundo.

–Entonces, ¿dónde podremos comer? –preguntó Alma.

–Vayan a "Cocina las ollitas", en la calle Dieciocho –intervino una abuelita–, la comida es muy buena y le pagan a sus trabajadores sueldos dignos. Ahí no hay ningún señor MacMann llenándose los bolsillos cada vez que alguien compra una hamburguesa.

–Esa me parece una muy buena idea –dijo la mamá.

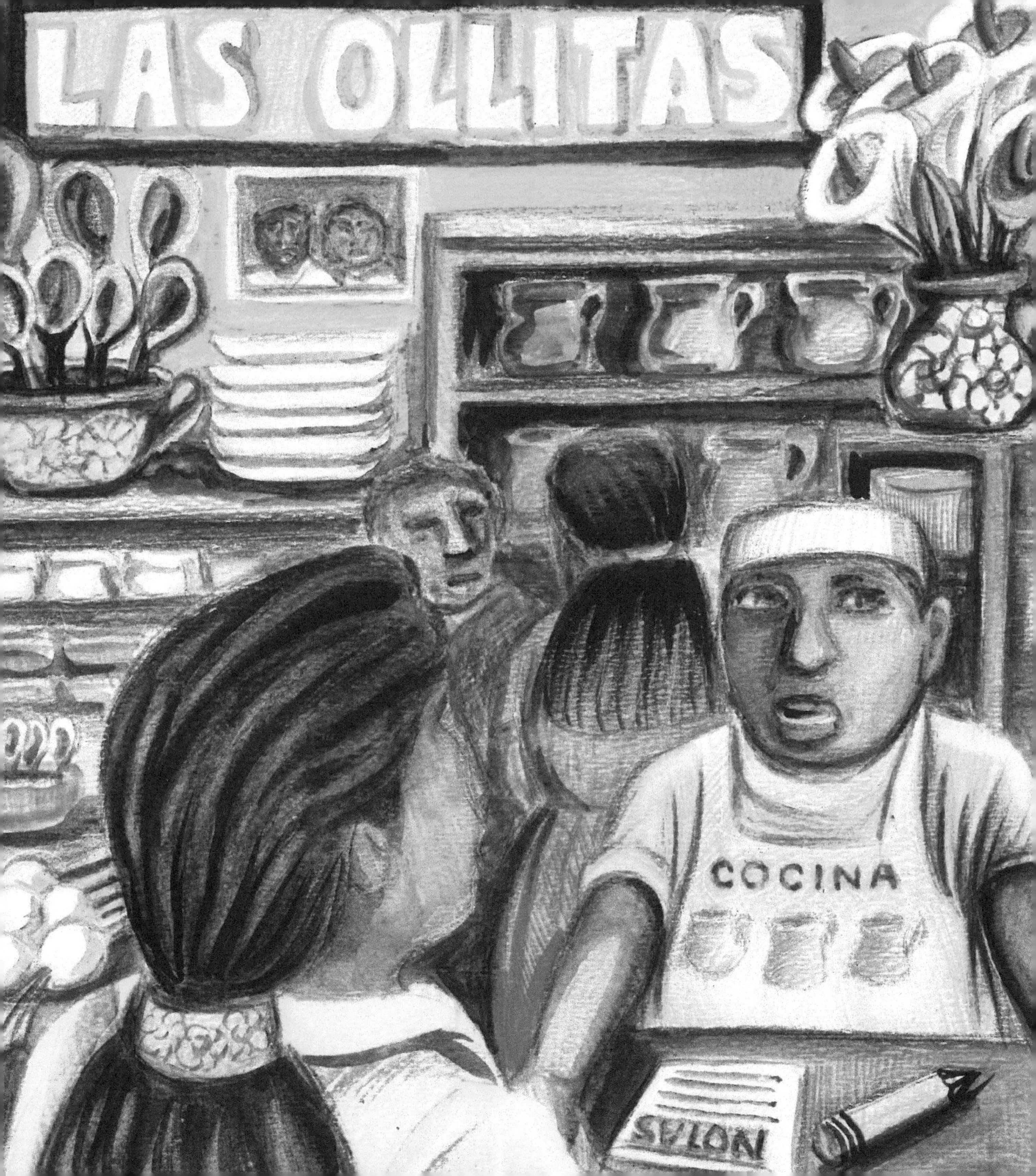
LAS OLLITAS
COCINA
NOTAS

The crowd was growing larger as men and women coming home from work joined in.

"Let's go, Joelito," said Papa. "You're the one who was so hungry."

Joelito just stood there lost in thought. He felt hunger in his belly, but he was feeling something else, too.

"I'm going to stay here with Brandon and Kayla," he said.

"Then I'm staying, too," said Alma. "Could you bring back take-out for us and for the Thomases?"

El grupo de gente crecía porque se unían a la protesta varios hombres y mujeres después de salir de sus propios trabajos.

–Bueno, Joelito, ¿nos vamos? Tú tenías más hambre que nadie.

Joelito permaneció parado, perdido en sus pensamientos. Sentía hambre en su panza; pero también sentía otra cosa, una emoción fuerte que venía de le gente unida, de las pancartas, de la pasión del señor Thomas, de la historia de sus abuelos.

–Voy a quedarme con Brandon y Kayla, papá –dijo Joelito con voz firme y espontánea.

–Entonces yo también me quedo –agregó Alma.

–¿Por qué mejor no van ustedes dos –le dijo Joelito a sus padres–, y nos traen algo de comer a nosotros y a la familia de Brandon?

As the sky cleared, the setting sun cast a shadow over Sam MacMann's plastic head, transforming his smile into a frown.

When Joelito and Alma joined the Thomas family, Kayla handed each of them a sign on a stick. The crowd began chanting, "Hey, hey, ho, ho, low wages have got to go!"

Joelito began chanting, too. He felt a new kind of joy as he realized all the people there were making history together.

Al caer la tarde, el cielo se despejó y la luz del atardecer cayó sobre la cabeza de plástico de Sam MacMann. Por unos instantes la sonrisa eterna de Sam se transformó en un gesto molesto.

Cuando Joelito y Alma se acercaron a la familia Thomas, Kayla les entregó una pancarta a cada uno. La multitud empezó a gritar: ¡Salarios dignidad! ¡Salarios dignidad! ¡Salarios dignidad!

Joelito se unió al coro y sintió una forma de alegría nunca antes experimentada, una alegría que venía, sin lugar a dudas, de la unión de la gente, de la clara sensación de estar haciendo historia juntos.

What Happened Next?

After one of many classroom discussions about *Joelito's Big Decision*, a sixth grader asked, "Well, what happened?" At first I thought he was confused about the plot. But that was not his question. He wanted to know what happened as a result of the demonstration. Did Mr. MacMann pay up?

I started writing *Joelito's Big Decision* in the fall of 2013, when the 21st Century movement to raise the minimum wage was just getting off the ground. Now, two years later, we can say that a lot happened, although there is still a very long way to go. There were demonstrations in support of raising the minimum wage in 190 cities on December 4, 2014. By March 2015 several cities and 24 states had voted to raise the minimum wage in 2015. The demand to raise the minimum wage has spread from fast food to Walmarts, home care workers, and federal contract and other workers.

However, of the 24 states, only one has raised the minimum above $10 an hour, hardly a living wage, and 95 percent of recent income increases have gone to the 1%.

On April 15, 2015 a million people across the US demonstrated in support of a living wage. It was the largest demonstration of its kind in history.

For further background information and ideas for teaching, see *Joelito's Big Decision* on the homepage of Hardball Press - www.hardballpress.com.

¿Qué pasó después?

Después de una de muchas discusiones en el aula sobre "La gran decisión de Joelito", un estudiante de sexto grado me preguntó: "Pero luego ¿qué pasó?" Al principio pensé que el estudiante estaba confundido con la historia, que no había entendido bien la trama; pero lo cierto es que esa pregunta no estaba enfocada en lo que ocurría en el libro sino en lo que ocurrió como consecuencia de la protesta. Es decir, ¿Les pagó el señor MacMann, sí o no?

Empecé a escribir "La Gran decisión de Joelito" cuando el movimiento del siglo XXI para aumentar el salario mínimo estaba empezando a despegar, era el otoño de 2013. Ahora, dos años después, podemos decir que han pasado muchas cosas importantes, pero que aún queda un largo camino por recorrer.

El 4 de diciembre de 2014 hubo manifestaciones en apoyo del aumento del salario mínimo en 190 ciudades de Estados Unidos. En marzo de 2015 se votó en varias ciudades y 24 estados para aumentar el salario mínimo en el año 2015. Sin embargo, de los 24 estados sólo uno ha subido el salario mínimo por encima de diez dólares por hora, un salario que aún no es justo ni digno para vivir. Además, el 95 por ciento de los recientes aumentos de ingresos han sido solo de uno por ciento.

Por otro lado, la demanda para aumentar el salario mínimo se ha extendido de la industria de comida rápida a los trabajadores de Walmart, a los trabajadores del hogar, a los trabajadores con contratos federales y a otros.

El 15 de abril de 2015, un millón de personas en los Estados Unidos salieron a las calles en apoyo de un salario digno para vivir. Esta ha sido la manifestación más grande de su tipo en la historia.

Para más información e ideas para la enseñanza, vea "La gran decisión de Joelito" en la página web de Hardball Press.

Ann Berlak has been a teacher and teacher educator for over fifty years. She believes schools should be places where children learn to become active creators of a more just and joyful world. She now writes fiction intended to spark thought and conversations about the injustices children and young people experience and to show how people working together can bring another better world into being. *Joelito's Big Decision* is her first children's book..

Daniel Camacho currently lives and works in Oakland, California. His at-home studio is filled with ongoing projects, and is usually open to visitors upon request. He teaches art to elementary and middle school students and works to promote an awareness of Mexican / Latino culture thru his participation with the Oakland Museum of California, the Spanish Speaking Unity Council, local public libraries and other community based organization.

José Antonio Galloso was born in Lima, Peru. He is a writer, photographer and a bilingual teacher with studies in audiovisual communication, Spanish and writing. He has published poetry and fiction and his works have been included in several anthologies. His photographic work, which he considers an extension of his writing, has been exhibited and published in different galleries, printed media and online. He has been living in the Bay Area since 2002. (Photo by Peskador)

TEACHING FOR SOCIAL JUSTICE

"If we can teach children about the transformation of a caterpillar into a butterfly, can we not teach them about transforming our social world into a more just and peaceful community?"

For thirty years I taught prospective elementary school teachers. My primary intention was to challenge the students to think about what kind of future they wanted to construct through what they taught. What should schooling in their classrooms be *for*, beyond preparing children to be "college and career ready"?

After retiring, I went back into classrooms as a guest social justice teacher. My adventures confirmed my belief that when given any encouragement at all, children and young people will eagerly engage in dialogue about the social, political, and economic issues that surround and shape them.

Eventually, I decided to write a story book for children that would help teachers and parents spark lively conversations like the ones I engaged in as a social justice teacher. The result was *Joelito's Big Decision/La gran decisión de Joelito*. To my great satisfaction, reading *Joelito* with or to children and young people often evokes those looks of surprise, the kind of "ah-ha" responses that are the true rewards every teacher cherishes.

Shouldn't we let children know that economic injustice and social activism did not end with Cesar Chavez and Dolores Huerta?

We hope that literary gatekeepers—parents, teachers, caregivers, and librarians—will share stories with children that depict ordinary people working together toward a better future. The bookshelves in our classrooms, libraries and homes are crowded with the tales of solitary heroes and heroines fighting battles in worlds of fantasy, mystery, and historical fiction. Stories of contemporary people in the struggle for social change belong on those bookshelves, too.

At what age should we begin talking with young children about economic justice and inequality?

Are elementary school children too young to think about social and political issues? Should we interfere with their innocence by prematurely exposing them to the darker sides of life?

- Which children are we talking about here? Certainly not those children who already experience economic hardship and uncertainty, or those who go to bed hungry because their parents can't find jobs that pay a living wage. Acknowledging these realities means acknowledging the experiences of children who are often marginalized in school and in children's fiction.

- When adults are silent about the social, political, and economic injustices in their community, children may internalize the perspectives that dominate public conversation. They may come to believe, for example, that people get rich because they are smarter or work harder. They may learn to blame the victim and to normalize war, violence and economic oppression.

- Keeping silent about social wrongs is disastrous for privileged children as well as for those who live in poverty and economic insecurity. Both groups drift toward the belief that this is how things have always been and will always be. Once established in childhood, these convictions can become resistant to change.

What stories should we share with young children?

Stories that reveal

- how the decisions and actions of each of us affect the lives and actions of others, often in hidden ways

- how differences of power in the hierarchies of race, class, gender, sexual orientation, and disability—differences that may be initially invisible—affect how we and other experience our lives differently (empathy)

- how to connect the dots between everyday injustices and the social forces that create and sustain them—for example, societal dynamics that create the vast extremes of wealth and poverty

- how ordinary people acting together can create a more just and joyful world

- that joining with others to create a more just future is a joyful life option for each of us

Some questions to pose to children before reading or listening to *Joelito*:

- Do you know anyone who can't find a job or works full time or even two jobs and still doesn't make enough money to buy what the family needs?

- Have you ever seen or been at a demonstration where people were trying to get someone or something to change? What did they want? Did they get it? (Ask your mom and dad or a friend if they have ever gone to a demonstration. Send out a questionnaire about it to another class.)

Prompts for large or small group discussions of Joelito

- Early in the story, Kayla gets angry with Joelito and tells him, "You don't understand anything." What did she mean? How important is it that he understand?

- Brandon's father explains to Joelito that Mr. McMann has "a billion dollars in the bank," while Brandon's father has no money saved. Does Mr. McMann have so much money because he worked a "billion" times harder than Brandon's mom and dad? What could be other reasons why he is so much richer than both Brandon's and Joelito's parents?

- Compare how much money the workers at MacMann's earn in an hour or a year to how much Mr. MacMann earns. Why does Mr. MacMann pay the workers so little?

- Joelito found many workers standing outside of MacMann's chanting, "Hey, hey, ho, ho, low wages have got to go!" Why do you think they carried signs and made a lot of noise? If they asked politely and quietly for more money, do you think Mr. MacMann would be more likely to raise their pay?

- How do you feel about the fact that a few people have lots and lots of money, and many who work for rich people have very little?

- Imagine you are Mr. McMann's son or daughter. You live in a big mansion, with servants who cook and clean up for the family. If you lived like that would you ever think about children who are hungry? Do you think the government should pass laws to make rich people share some of their wealth with poorer people?

- If the workers work hard but make too little money to support their families, what can they do about it?

- Is there any place in the world where everyone has a home and enough to eat? And everyone can go to the doctor for free? Is that even possible?

Important basics you will have to teach along the way

You may prepare for a discussion about the possibilities for reducing inequalities of wealth or income by teaching the notions of *the commons, public* institutions and *taxes* or you can teach them along the way. I have found that most children have no idea of who owns public schools or public libraries, or what the words public, the commons and taxes mean.

Online research

Search for groups of workers that are fighting for a higher minimum wage. Find photos of many varied demonstrations in the US and elsewhere. Older students can consult websites that give statistics on the distributions of wealth and income.

Post reading activity

Put students in groups of four and have them agree upon a business they would like to start. The business will pay $16,000 in wages to four workers each month.

The teacher appoints one person "boss" and then asks the students to decide the roles each of the three others plays in that business (i.e. making the product, selling it, shipping it, etc.) and how they would divide up the $16, 000 they have for monthly wages among the four. How much more should the boss make than the workers? Older children can compare the ratio of earnings between workers and "bosses" they agreed on to the ratio in the US and in several other countries, and discuss the pros and cons of various distributions of income.

Promoting deeper discussion

- Listen carefully to, and help children and young people clarify, their questions.

- Ask children and young people to what extent they agree with something someone else has said and why. Or what they think others who are not present might think. (Don't just move on to another question after one answer or viewpoint has been offered.)

- Ask groups of three or four children to see if they can agree on an answer to a question, and if not, to report dominant and minority opinions to the class.

Listening to children and young people's views will reveal the meanings they have constructed from observing and eavesdropping upon the adult world. Listening to how children and young people view their world will open adults' eyes to the complex social and economic understandings and misunderstanding children and young people have internalized.

Most important, adults will discover that children want to understand their political and social worlds.

For further information and teaching ideas see *Joelito's Big Decision* on Facebook, and on the Hardball Press homepage www.hardballpress.com. You may also e-mail me at anncberlak@yahoo.com.

CPSIA information can be obtained
at www.ICGtesting.com
Printed in the USA
LVHW071609180821
695592LV00024B/2352